From DAD

9/1/91

Every Kid's Guide to
Watching TV
Intelligently

Written by

JOY BERRY

CHILDRENS PRESS ®
CHICAGO

About the Author and Publisher

Joy Berry's mission in life is to help families cope with everyday problems and to help children become competent, responsible, happy individuals. To achieve her goal, she has written over two hundred self-help books for children from birth through age twelve. Her work revolutionized children's publishing by providing families with practical, how-to, living skills information that was previously unavailable in children's books.

Joy gathered a dedicated team of experts, including psychologists, educators, child developmentalists, writers, editors, designers, and artists, to form her publishing company and to help produce her work.

The company, Living Skills Press, produces thoroughly researched books and audio-visual materials that successfully combine humor and education to teach subjects ranging from how to clean a bedroom to how to resolve problems and get along with other people.

Managing Editor: Ellen Klarberg
Copy Editor: Kate Dickey
Contributing Editors: Libby Byers, Nancy Cochran, Maureen Dryden, Yona Flemming, Kathleen Mohr, Susan Motycka
Editorial Assistant: Sandy Passarino

Art Director: Laurie Westdahl
Design: Abigail Johnston, Laurie Westdahl
Production: Abigail Johnston
Illustrations designed by: Bartholomew
Inker: Berenice Happe Iriks
Colorer: Berenice Happe Iriks
Composition: Curt Chelin

No matter who you are, chances are that you watch TV. You probably began watching TV at a very early age. By the time you graduate from high school, you probably have spent 15,000 hours watching TV.

In **EVERY KID'S GUIDE TO WATCHING TV INTELLIGENTLY** you will learn the following:

- why watching TV can be harmful,
- how watching TV can be helpful,
- how to watch TV moderately,
- how to watch TV safely,
- how to choose the right programs to watch, and
- how to respond to TV commercials.

Many concerned adults think that watching too much TV can harm you.

TV can cause you to think things that are not true.

TV can influence you to want things that are not good for you.

Watching TV can take the place of spending time with friends and other people.

Watching TV can take the place of doing creative things.

Watching TV can cause you to become a "watcher" instead of a "doer." It can keep you from doing other things.

Watching TV can cause you to run away from your problems instead of solving them.

TV can influence you to do things that are not good for you or others.

TV can influence you to become too aggressive or even violent.

If it is true that watching TV can be harmful, should you stop watching?

A TV is only an electrical appliance. It is neither good nor bad.

It is how you use a TV that is good or bad.

Watching TV can help you if you use it properly.
TV can help you relax and unwind.

TV can be entertaining.

TV can expose you to new ideas.

TV can broaden your view of the world.

TV can teach you valuable information.

TV can stimulate interesting conversations between
you and others.

Too much of anything is not good for a person. This is true of watching TV. Thus, you must not watch too much TV if you want it to be helpful instead of harmful.

Some people say that young people should not watch more than one hour of TV a day. Others say that young people can watch TV up to four hours a day.

No matter what other people say, you and your parents or guardians must decide how much TV you will watch. It might be one, two, three, or four hours a day.

Whatever you and your parents or guardians decide, remember it is not good for you
- to watch more than four hours of TV a day or
- to watch TV for more than two hours at one time.

Here are five rules you must follow while watching TV. They will help you avoid straining your eyes or damaging your eardrums.

Rule 1. Do not sit too close to the TV while you are watching it.

Measure the width of your TV screen. Multiply the width by five. This will tell you how far away you should sit from your TV when you watch it.

Rule 2. Do not wear sunglasses while you
watch TV.

Rule 3. Do not watch TV in a completely dark room.

Rule 4. Do not put the TV where you will see glare or reflections from lights or windows.

Rule 5. Do not turn the sound above a normal listening level while you are watching TV.

In addition to following these rules, it is important to use the TV set carefully.

It is an electrical appliance and can give you an electrical shock if not handled properly.

Some TV programs are suitable for you to watch while others are not. With the help of your parents or guardians, you can decide which programs are suitable and which are not by asking yourselves certain questions.

Question 1. Do I find the program interesting or entertaining?

Question 2. Is the program something I can understand?

Question 3. Does the program make clear what is real and what is unreal?

Question 4. Will the program frighten or upset me in any way?

Question 5. Will the program help me understand and appreciate myself and the world around me?

Question 6. Does the program teach values that will help me be a good person?

Question 7. Does the program put crime and violence in proper perspective?

- Crime and violence should not be presented as good or right.
- Crime should never win over law and order.
- Violence should never be shown as a way to solve problems.

Question 8. Will the program encourage me to do healthy, worthwhile activities instead of harmful, destructive ones?

These questions need to be answered *before* you watch a program. It might be helpful if you and your parents or guardians look through a TV schedule at least once a week. Using the eight questions as a guideline, decide which programs would be good for you to watch.

Mark the programs you and your parents or
guardians have chosen. Make a note of the times
they will be shown. Turn on the TV just before each
program begins. Then turn it off when each
program ends. Try not to turn on the TV at any
other time.

It costs a lot of money to make a TV program. The money comes from sponsors. A sponsor is usually a company that wants to sell something.

A sponsor gets the attention of thousands of people by showing a program on TV. While people are watching the program, the sponsor interrupts with a commercial.

A commercial is a message that tries to convince people to buy something.

Some commercials are made especially for you. These commercials try to persuade you to buy such things as food, drinks, candy, games, toys, and clothes. Even though you might not be able to buy the product yourself, the sponsor hopes you will convince your parents or guardians to buy it for you.

Some commercials use special words, sound effects, music, lighting, and photography to make a product look better than it is.

These commercials can trick you into buying
products that are not good products. They can trick
you into buying products that are not suitable
for you.

Before you buy a product that has been advertised on TV, find out all you can about it.

Read the label before you buy any product that you are going to eat or drink. Decide whether the contents will be good or bad for you. You might need to ask an adult to help you with this decision.

Here are some helpful questions to ask before you buy a toy or game that is advertised on TV:

1. Does the item look good to me? Is it something I really want?
2. Will the item work? Will it do what it is supposed to do?
3. How long will the item last? Is it strong enough to take normal wear?
4. Can I use the item in more than one way? Will it stimulate my thinking, creativity, or physical activity?
5. Can I use the item by myself, or will I need a lot of help from an adult?
6. Is the item safe?

Here are some guidelines for choosing safe toys:
Safe toys

- can be cleaned,
- will not burn easily,
- will not cause allergies,
- are not poisonous,
- do not have sharp points or edges,
- do not have pinch places such as springs or hinges,
- do not have small parts that can be swallowed by a younger child, and
- will not give an electrical shock.

Watching TV is like anything else. It can be good or bad for you. It all depends on how you use it.